Last of the Marlboro Men
ISBN 978-1-7782810-0-6
Copyright ©2022 Scott A. Hamilton
https://scottahamilton.com

Cover art by Scott A. Hamilton ©2022

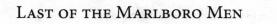

LAST OF THE MARLBORO MEN

CONTENTS

PART 1: ROOTS

PART 2: OF GODS AND MEN

PART 3: THE LOVE POEMS

PART 4: LAST OF THE MARLBORO MEN

PART 5: REQUIEM

Dedicated to my children: Josh, Nathan, Lydia and Mika.

PART 1

ROOTS

*(When we are young,
with what scale do we measure ourselves?)*

CHILDHOOD MEMORIES OF CLIMBING AN APPLE TREE

she beckons with hovering grace,
dancing post blossom in the warm wind.

her cloven trunk
gives sure purchase for my feet;

split where the great tree groans in the wind.
I push up to her beckoning branches,

where her gnarled hands toss me skyward
into my canopy bed.

there I recline,
plucking sour fruit,

pretending to be Dionysus
tended by fawning leaves.

PINPRICKS OF LIGHT

There is an underexposed photo, taken
at my sixth birthday party.
The candles burn bright spots
in the emulsion, my eyes two pinpricks of light.
Others, caught in the flash,
curl around the edges of the print. They
lack significance or meaning—they are
faceless cake-eaters, players
in a childish theatre long forgotten.

I remember the cake had a wax paper wrapped
quarter inside, revealed in a slice-and-serve
game of Russian roulette (won fairly by
a faceless Special Boy that was not me). I remember
a cold November draft from the porch door
that had caused the candles to flutter.

Sounds float out of the old photo:
the pot-bellied Quebec heater crackles
against a late Ontario winter; the laughter of
child actors reverberates in the soundboard
of the old upright piano in the kitchen corner;
mother coaxing me to play my part. (I knew
even then that I was the blood of an
uneven pact, sum of an odd mismatch
steeped in dysfunction, in a country
far too large to be close to anything.)

I was the youngest, always sensitive,
naive and lacking savvy for my six years.
(I always felt tolerated rather than liked.)
I tried to be part of things but
could never quite connect; I remember
wishing I could sink through the linoleum floor
to hide out in the earthen basement until
the party guests had all gone home.

Mother, ever present, always tried to be my beacon.

OBJECTS FROM MY YOUTH

(IN THE ORDER THEY CAME TO MIND)

'74 Pinto station wagon,
   red with running boards painted black to hide the rust.
   (I beat a Mustang once in a cross-town race to Bino's.)

A marionette I made in school,
   paper-mache head, macabre Mardi Gras effigy,
   articulated dowelled legs in poorly-stitched clothes.

A Millennium Falcon model,
   cockpit lit up like a holiday decoration,
   hung above my dresser in mock flight.

The bow and arrow I ashamedly used
   to pierce a pigeon's nest high in the barn rafters.
   (Father had to climb up to retrieve the arrow.)

Father's handmade leather knife case
   he wore on his belt every day; it smelled of him
   for years after he was gone.

The orange spun-plastic globe fixture,
   married perfectly with the pale azure walls of my bedroom.
   It was the world I orbited every night as I went to sleep.

A copy of *Tom Swift in the Race to the Moon,*
   The Chronicles of Narnia, Watership Down,
   piles of comics: D.C., Marvel, Weird Science and
   Haunted Tank, (with the German speech bubbles
   translated to English in the caption below).

Hot Wheels with errant wobbly axle pins,
   (never rolled straight for racing).

Blue rabbit; velvety fur.

VENATIONE

What a sight:
Mother, rainsuit and rubber gloves
taped at the cuff,
(I don't remember what she had on her head)
a can of RAID and a flyswatter her sword and shield,
inflicting carnage on an army of rogue bees.

My brother stands in the distance, small and shirtless,
frozen loaves of bread soothing the welts on his torso,
watching his gladiatrix fight for honour.

RAY

We lived across the road from Mary and Wally Maclean (not husband and wife but elderly siblings). Mary made wonderful apple pie, and their ducks would sometimes wander up our driveway.

Their nephew Raymond came to stay one summer. With thick red hair and a ruddy face, he didn't look to me like he was from the city. He was older than my brother, who idolized him. Ray had those kind of eyes that wouldn't rest, and even I knew in my boyhood naivety that he saw my brother as a vessel to corrupt simply to assuage his own captive boredom.

I dreaded going with them but mother said they had to take me, that I shouldn't always be left behind; she always had the best intentions.

Our corner of rural Ontario had very straight gravel roads and I trudged along after them forever, choking on swirls of dust left by passing cars, feeling small and invisible.

An abandoned barn became unlikely entertainment; there had been ducks there once as well. Ray and my brother lit up a Colts cigarillo, the kind with the sweet tasting plastic filter tip, and suddenly I was no longer invisible. I had become the unlikely entertainment as I coughed and hacked on my best effort to fit in.

But sport to boys intent on misadventure is fleeting; a new game ensued as I became a moving target, which left me to walk all the way back home alone, reeking of rotten duck eggs hardening in the sun.

I stood under the shower for an eternity, clothes and all, crying, not knowing if I should be more angry with my brother or my mother for making them take me, or if I would be the one in trouble for ruining my clothes.

But no matter how hard I tried, no matter how long I soaked or scrubbed, the rotten smell of my smallness just wouldn't wash off.

SSP RACERS

I remember the short loop green carpet
on the floor of the family room addition
and the warped sheet of half inch plywood
that covered the cellar stairs at one end.

The carpet was perfect for Hot Wheels cars;
they'd make it all the way to the far wall,
each car with its own unique curving trajectory
to the left or the right.

My brother and I placed stacks of comics
as goal posts,
to see who could get the most cars through.
As in most things, he usually won.

Christmas '75 brought our racing to new heights
when we both opened our gifts
(it had to be simultaneous to not ruin the surprise)
—a pair of Kenner SSP racers.

Gloriously weighty in the hand
due to the rubber-tyred gyro wheel,
they were virtually indestructible
and would go as fast as you could pull the zip cord.

My brother got the Super Stocker Superbird
with the signature tail fin;
mine was the sleek and futuristic King Cobra
in glorious metallic green.

We started on the family room carpet,
propping up the plywood over the cellar hole
to see how far we could launch them
and still get them to land on their wheels.

Eventually we backed all the way down the hall
and into the kitchen
to see whose car could make it the farthest
without crashing into a door frame.

We raced for the entire school break that year,
the sonic whine of twin spinning gyros
echoing endlessly
through our old brick farmhouse.

The next year my brother was too old for toy cars.
He hung out more with his hockey friends
and I moved on to model building;
something I could do alone.

THEIR BOY TOMMY

There is a photo of my mother laughing,
her young eyes bright as diamonds, taken at
the Lauther's new year's party in Cobourg
where we spent the weekend that year.

Their boy Tommy, who was my age,
preferred my older brother and laughed
during our backyard misadventures
at my awkward, face-down muddy expense.

I remember hiding before midnight, not
wanting to celebrate anything. Perhaps it was
because of Tommy; me resenting having to
wear his clothes while mine were in the wash,

or perhaps it was some kind of enlightenment,
that face-down muddy feeling
casting omens about the long move west
when our home was to become an exile,

about how it would be one of the last times
I would hear my mother laugh out loud
in that sparkling, carefree way,
her young eyes bright as diamonds.

THINGS THAT DIDN'T WORK OUT

Kites never stayed afloat for me
no matter how fast I ran;
tangled string and cheap ripped plastic
dragging and bouncing along the hard earth.

Balsa wood model plane,
elastic propeller engine overwound in
a desperate attempt at meaningful flight;
wing smashed along with my optimism.

Model radio built in our dirt basement
(wrapping wire carefully, attaching
battery with hope of my own connection)
all for dead air—not even static.

So I gave up on engineering or connection at eight,
relegated myself to a tradesman's life
gluing and painting static model cars and
Lego; thank God for Lego.

CANADIAN DREAM

When my family moved across Canada, I saw
for the first time never-ending roads straight
as the lines on foolscap paper, while our friends
faded out of the rear window of our Chevy Malibu.

It was the month *O Canada* became the official
national anthem, marking a birthday of sorts,
and the month Terry Fox passed by our home town.

My father, too, was chasing a dream;
a horse-buggy adorned the top of our tent trailer,
laden with the intention of finding the Wild West.

The rest of our home bounced along precariously in boxes
past a thousand lakes and across the Rocky Mountains,
all the provincial campsites blurring together as one.

My brother and I were relieved to see the snow-capped peaks
in the distance, slowly revealed as the curvature
of the earth rolled up the last of the prairies.

'There it is,' our father had said. But the marker that read
WELCOME TO BRITISH COLUMBIA held no fanfare,
only the beginning of a new foreboding wilderness,

and after my brother left and memories of home
slowly disappeared in the coming years, purged from
still-packed boxes onto flea market tables,

it felt like our journey west never ended
as our family became lost in that wilderness
in search of a particular kind of Canadian Dream.

ELO

My brother and I slept upstairs
in the open loft of the 575 square foot cabin
we'd helped our father build.
The loft was also our gym, our lookout for
wildlife in the back fields and our refuge
from our new unplugged life,
having moved over 4000 kilometers
across a country that swallows families
to watch our father become a bear.
We clung to the small gas-powered generator
that we were allowed to run an hour a day after school,
and under the light of kerosene lanterns in winter
life surged into our little loft as our salvaged
record player began to spin, and April Wine,
Queen and ELO streamed out of Radio Shack speakers
like medicine, transporting us back to a life of
modern convenience just for a moment.
But occasionally the music would falter
as the generator ran out of gas, and as
ELO's *Don't Bring Me Down* slowed in pitch and tempo,
eventually grinding to a halt,
our momentary escape ended, bringing on
the eerie silence of British Columbian backwoods,
which was almost too loud for us to take.

NORTH

diesel and sawdust
chainsaw smoke and kerosene

bear's teeth from a carcass in the back field
fences down from a startled moose

moving the neighbor's cattle to the next pasture
making butter

getting the chores list done
free time running through the woods

impossibly big skies
long sunny days

learning to skin a grouse
riding dirt bikes to the lake

the smell of horse sweat and leather
endless brown carpet of aspen leaves

walking to the highway to catch the school bus
the sound of snow that squeaks when you step on it

firewood piled up to the roof
bedsheets frozen stiff on the clothesline

tobogganing at the gravel pit up the road
icy plumes of breath

burning fingers from the cold
melting boots too close to the fire

the hiss of propane lights
breaking the ice in the well with the rope & pail

cracked seat in the outhouse
dancing skies at midnight

grey-brown late winter thaw
the smell of new spring

I remember North

PROPANE LIGHTS IN WINTER

glowing trees and moon-blue fields,
auroras borealis holding celestial court

amber cast of propane lights,
shadows etched into the ceiling

memories as faded photographs
(the old mill wears a white shawl)

Father with an armload of firewood,
face obscured by dancing snow

THE DOCK AT OSCAR LAKE

lost memories between brothers:

brown mink baring
teeth, hissing minatory;

solitary snap of skull, then—
an empty skin, stretched, eyeless,

hanging lifeless in dad's tool shed
smelling of death and fear

a hideous reminder of
our first murder

GROWING UP COLD

The floors in our house were always cold;
a square block of concrete that never warmed,
even when the woodstove glowed red.

No matter how high we stacked birch or fir,
no number of blankets; nothing dulled the chill
once winter settled in to our home.

Mother spread sweeping compound everywhere
and swept repeatedly; I think now that maybe
it was to keep her heart from freezing.

THE ROCKING CHAIR

My father's early inheritance sat for years
upon the coiled red rug my mother had made.
Not significant in itself, it had hints of Scandinavian lines
with low-profile rockers and sweat-stained slanted arms,
the seat trimmed in cracked brown Naugahyde,

a classic from the Sears catalogue
back when that was fashionable.
If it weren't for the stalwart rug
my father would likely have worn through the floor
rocking back and forth, lost to us in an endless supply

of flea-market paperback westerns
for days at a time.
I didn't understand the nature of his silence;
he seemed resentful of our existence
although I was sure I hadn't done anything wrong.

The first real revelation came
when we traveled back east
and I met my grandfather, for the second time.
He had the matching chair
except trimmed in green,

the finish on the unprotected floor below it
worn through in two distinct grooves.
He had the same eyes as well,
the kind that look at you
while seeing something off in the distance,
as if something better was there.

LAMENT IN FOUR LINES

Blurred vision

<On the trip home his chest tightened> Mother said

When he came to the city for scans

I was too busy to go see him

*(And then reality sidestepped; a lapse
in the course of things meant to be.)*

THE SILENCE BEARS WITNESS TO MY FATHER'S DEATH

JULY 30, 1988, HWY 97 SOUTH: 1 AM

A sudden deconstruction;
glass bursting into stars in a night sky,
recreating the Milky Way.

Concrete and antifreeze and oil and blood
compress to form a new compound,
hard and slick and unforgiving.

Metal and plastic and bone disassemble
and reassemble into foreign shapes
to the slow beat of an unfamiliar percussion.

Punctuation marks
at the end of a black rubber cursive
long enough to contain a lifetime.

Under the earth,
nightcrawlers reach up,
feeling the vibration of rain.

Above, poplars exhale.
A slight ruffle of feathers as an owl
turns its head.

The sound is no more than
a momentary prick of ear
or fluttering eyelash for a nearby doe;

a stirring of air
for the wild things
going about their existence.

As a flower furls for the cold night,
so does the man
as he, too, becomes quiet.

LONG DRIVE HOME

the year ended abruptly at 6 am that july day
with a foreboding wail of the phone

     hullo?

a ragged silence hung on the line
until my brother choked out my name

I knew, then, already
and I said,

     who?

it was a long drive home
and for me
the leaves had already fallen,

leaving ashes in their wake

MOTHER, JULY 1988

The unpredicted,
disbelieved;
the numb.
The brother,
driving home together in
the coffin that was his '70 Nova.

The cop:
<youbeendrinkin, son?>

But he'd heard about the
accident on his police radio;
the early morning crash, the fire.
He let us go with a mercy warning,
as long as I drove.

The twitchy clutch.

Mom.
We'd gone up to be with her, but
she is mostly absent from
my memory of that day, except for
the fight,
her intervention between brothers.
He: the embattled, the bitter.
Me: the too young, the naive, the lost.
We brought her to
even more tears.

Me, not knowing
how to be a real person,
doing my best to become a ghost, a spectre;
avoid the swell of houseguests,
disappear, find a hole.

We'd gone up to be with Mother,
and I don't even remember her being there.

My father's casket yawned,
a toothless grin, crooning
Hey Kid, Just Kidding
to the tune of an old Hank Williams song.

There, lying static in the ruffled mouth, was
a poor replica of the man, like something
from a Madame Tussaud's museum or
one of those B-level horror flicks.

My brother bent his face inside
and kissed the waxen effigy on its forehead,
thinking it was the real thing
while I recoiled in absolute terror of laughing aloud

but I clung tightly to my lamentation mask, and as
Clowns & Spectres danced in the funeral parlour lobby
I remember the last lesson my father would ever teach me:
that grief is an unpredictable bastard.

DON'T WORRY

At the funeral
the pastor spoke of a conversation
he'd had with my father
to assuage any fear of damnation:
'Don't worry, Lance, I believe in
Jesus as my saviour,'
he quoted my dad as saying.

Even as I heard the words
I could feel the cruel backhand of
my Baptist grandmother, the snarl of
her thin-lipped maternal office
ripping through any hope for
his childhood authenticity or
chance of real love,
or, by inheritance, mine.

I leaned back in the hard pew,
crossed my legs,
and nodded at the irony.

FUNERALS

So many flowers.

So many flowers left behind
from well-wishers, feel-gooders,
so-sorry-for-your-lossers.

They tumble out of church doors,
filling the backs of cars with
picked-over trays of food spilling
sloppy sentiments into mothers' kitchens.

The dead flowers, once finished mockery,
go in the bin in the end, looking like
feathers ripped from roosters in a hurricane.

Perhaps next time we can do it in reverse:
serve cold cockerel meat,
gift everyone a red feather while
the congregation sings *I'll Fly Away*
backwards, slowly.

DIRT

what strange ghouls float
through Mother's kitchen
chewing sloppily on hasty hors d'oeuvres,
pious funeral masks painted except
for the odd one willing
to chance a laugh at Father's expense

Medusa slithers up with
rotting breath in my ear:
'He was an alcoholic you know.'
I dared not steal a glance toward the monster
but in turning away she caught my arm;

'They were headed for divorce as well,
he really wasn't a good husband.'

I pondered on her need to say it,
safe now he was dead

LOSS

I went to the scrap yard with my uncle
to examine Dad's 1985 Ford Tempo.
'Someone was threatening to sue,' he said,
so he had me take pictures as well.

The mangled car was barely recognizable,
paint and glass melted away in the inferno.
It was no longer blue, but the colour of
rust and an ashen sky.

The raw metal frames of his glasses on the floor of the front passenger side
hit me in the chest with a fist of familiarity;
a portrait without a face,
a ghost reaching out of empty eye sockets.

That was decades ago.
I still wish I'd have reached in and taken them
as a memento to his existence, or a talisman
against the sour irony of his own words:

'We are so tough, yet so fragile at the same time.'

WORK GLOVES

I have a photograph
of your work gloves sitting on a sawhorse.

They look as though your hands are still in them,
stained and hardened by sweat and sawdust,

permanently cast to the shape of you;

your strength and power dismembered,
still working while the rest of you disappeared.

I had just become an art school dropout,
ended my first live-in relationship,
watched my mother become a widow
and helped my family drift apart in three directions.

I learned much later that estrangement follows
relationships that can't define themselves
and also that young men can't survive on dreams,
so when cigarettes hit $3.25 a pack I quit those, too.

I found a used typewriter to keep my fingers busy,
re-examining my floundering faith in prose
and trying to place my responsibility in
others' expectations and failing to find it.

So I became a tradesman, just like my father.

But I missed the cigarettes, the sweet blue comfort,
my lungs still fresh enough to translate
the little nicotine buzz to my body; my non-judgemental
companion in a time of small deaths and endings.

CIGARETTES HIT $3.25 A PACK THAT YEAR

DARK, ALONE

As in the first memory of many things,
foundations upon which beliefs are built—

    [a spider's slow crooked knees]

it's possible to tap into those foundations,
deconstruct, lay them out in the sun,

    [first cry of terror, dark, trapped and alone]

analyze the reasons why so many of us built
upon traumatic findings,

    [long articulated legs reach into my crib]

that trauma brings a natural reflex of self
preservation, an indelible impression on the psyche;

    [Mother comes running]

still, fear is an excellent defence.

ALL THE NAMELESS SPIRITS

(Alfred turns, faceless
drops a bald stone in
witching pools
stealing futures not his own)

Her tiny, wrinkled face looked up at us
'Hi, I'm Minnie,' she smiled,
stretching out a delicate hand in introduction

(Alexander pats his cold chest
past lives line his pockets
forgotten dynasties
hearths without spark)

I saw for just an instant from
the corner of my eye
the sudden recognition of deep loss
in my mother's face, her gentle beauty
momentarily falling prostrate to
the ground in mourning,
along with a thousand memories of home

(Alistair tap dances gaily
a tune faintly familiar
brush & spank distorted
echoes of discomfort
ripples of gravity)

but then she caught herself,
straightened her shoulders and
forced a smile, accepting
my grandmother's outstretched hand,
choking out the words:

'Hi Minnie, I'm Marie.'

(Arthur looks on, slightly distant
tips his hat
standing in formation with
all the nameless spirits)

33

A KIND OF LOST

Waiting,
calculating futures by rearranging chairs
over and over again,
drawing border lines of regret,
wearing grooves in the floor.
(Everything and nothing looks familiar)

Waiting
for predetermination to allow me
to choose it and cut out my eyes
(my voice is different in my memory)
or until all of the mirrors fall to the floor,
so I can finally abolish reflection.
(Everything and nothing looks familiar)

Waiting, still,
weighing the silences we spoke in,
the shape of family heirlooms
that aren't family heirlooms at all,
but cobwebs and dust in holes.
(All of it and none of it looks familiar)

Waiting for originality
when all I hear is a warped signal
and all I see is a refraction of history;
voices from holes and inverted faces
staring up from resurrected boxes.
(Everything and nothing looks familiar)

Waiting for freedom
from an infinite number of choices,
any of which seem to lead in circles,
offering invitation to unfulfilled days
spent endlessly rearranging furniture.
(Everything and nothing will ever look familiar)

PART 2

OF GODS AND MEN

*(The masses stare blankly at the altar,
and God taps the mic:)*

<Is this thing even on?>

GODS AND MEN IN THE NEW AGE

Mortals
reroute the sun, placing it once again
securely in orbit around themselves.

Copernicus
shakes his head, sadly
rolling over in his grave.

Prometheus,
from his mountain prison, repeatedly
bites off his own hands in remorse.

FINDING GOD

I was nine when I stood at the front of the Wesley United Church on Rural Route Twelve, dressed in a white polyester robe awaiting baptism. The other three candidates up there with me were wailing babies held by their mothers, and I remembered wondering, through my conspicuous embarrassment, why they needed to be born again already.

One year later the man who baptised me sexually assaulted my father during a camping trip while he slept, and since that time I have known countless disappointments at the natural weakness of those who purported to be godly.

Now every poem I write is interpreted with biblical meaning by my mother. I don't take offense; I know it's how she understands things. But I have moved on to a greater examination of self and the mortal soul, the beautiful complexity of creatures loathe with built-in baggage.

I would like to know, however: is it considered anthropomorphization to assign God human attributes, or is it the other way around? Is 'He' open to interpretation, like we are?

MISSIONARY MAN

To the man at the front of the room
wielding wayward whelps like clay
making grandiose gestures and
false flowery prophesies:

you're just another giant mouth
smacking lies and eating the weak
to feed your godlike ego
greasing the gate-hinges of Sheol.

The pan flute at your lips pips
prepping potential converts;
'the harvest is ripe' lilts hollow with
no truth of kindness in your notes.

'Go forth and lay siege;
bring me the weak and the helpless!
Go and judge not yourselves, for
the dead are the dead already.'

CERRO AZUL

I motioned to my camera, asking for a photo.

The woman seemed slightly agitated but acquiesced,
obligated by the work we had done.

Later, upon developing the prints, I saw written
in her piercing eyes (and in the protective
hand over her children):

'We Are Not A Spectacle.'

TIJUANA

Dave loved gravel pits,
not young souls fresh
for shaping into hapless missionaries.

He drove our Suburban across the Mexican border
on angel wings and prayers; flaming
oil can road markers lit the Way

(he'd fitted the truck with an orange flashing light
to fool the Federales and smooth
our path to godly service).

On the third day he took two of the
hard-case girls into Tijuana to
'show them the other side' while

the rest of us put a roof on a church,
singing songs and eating mannah
the villagers pulled out of a hole.

After the return home there were
hushed phone calls, huggermugger,
something about Tijuana.

I still wonder if Dave ever opened his gravel pit.

UZBEKISTAN, 1992

Kutchkar, the goat.
That's how he was introduced,
most likely due to his wiry frame and sharp grey beard,
although he had the kindest eyes.

From him I learned the most:
how to walk barefoot in gravel without looking down,
how to take a mud bath in the waist-deep Lake Aydorkul
where fish grow suspiciously to greater than eight feet in length,
and how to slap stinging nettles on the back after a steam bath
for good health and increased blood flow.

Kutchkar was a happy man,
content with his life and his country.
Even though he spoke no English
and I could barely count to twenty in his language
I remember no barrier in communication.

Through him,
I remember communion
with a beautiful country.

OPEN MARKET, DJIZZAKH

A seller's nest of figs
snuggles sweetly in rows
like plump teeth blanketed
in a soft mouth of leaves.
Neighbouring sweet melons;
giant oval heads
bursting with the flavour
of Central Asian sun,
gently magnifying the scent
of fresh-baked soft golden naan
splayed like a deck of cards,
each dimple a signature
of the maker's hands.
The red meat also hangs, beckoning.
I counter the vendor's price in good faith—
<*yigirma besh*>, I say over the bustle;
the vendor makes a public show of
laying his knife on the weights,
(to rousing cheers)
gifting the choicest piece of fat.
I am a comedic sensation,
haggling over a price
everyone knows is reserved
only for me.

YURI

Yuri:
shock of red hair in a
black leather jacket,
dipping his toes in the tides of change,
desperate for a better life.
'Tell me what you need,' he said, 'I will get it for you.'
And he always did.
Black market mafia underground,
capital city,
Tashkent.

A celebration at the apartment block
for his young bride
Tonya,
with old records, darkened rooms and a disco ball
reminiscent of grade eight bashfulness
when hormones outweighed experience.
Her father Vasily,
happy to cook the food reserved for special occasions
and precariously chauffeur us
to and from the party in his Lada.

Yuri always had a pocket full of Canadian flag pins;
aspirations of a better existence
where water pipes don't burst without explanation
and books don't have to be sold out of the trunk of a car
in the fear that nothing will really change.

JUDAS ISCARIOTS

'America!' he said. I looked at him in surprise and replied, 'No, no, Canada!' pointing at the maple leaf pin that Yuri had given me. He laughed and clapped me on the shoulder. 'America!' he repeated. To him, there was no difference, and even though it made me feel a bit unsettled, perhaps he was right.

We were aliens there, having to learn simple things like to never shake the water off your hands after washing or settle on the first price stated for naan or gusht at the local market, or put a book on the floor. The men always greeted with a physical touch; the women, a polite nod.

The dinner invitation had been a roughly translated letter from their school age daughter, which manifested into a stressful four-hour drive in the ebbing darkness of early morning; a harrowing game of chicken on uneven and decaying roads. It was to become a collision of cultures in that, unbeknownst to us, the invitation was intended to be a three-day feast.

As is ancient tradition, our hosts had slaughtered their fattened calf and brought out a dazzling array of food of which only a fraction would be eaten; not refusing what was offered yet not eating too much became a learned skill. After eating, drinking, and a few culturally prescribed formalities that evening came the real reason we had been brought so far to their home. An impossible plea, presented with earnest hope through the sole English speaker in their company: to bring the daughter who had written the letter of invitation back to 'America', as if we were commanders of fate and the world power incarnate.

The fallen faces upon our reply, the hurt looks and disappointment from the women (outwardly, the men were stoic as roosters), somehow left us feeling a bit Judas Iscariot, even though we had been set up that way. The awkwardness was palpable after that, so with much discussion we convinced them that we could not stay any longer and said our goodbyes. The driver was gracious but clearly upset to make the return trip the same day.

We made it back to our quarters in the early hours of the morning, having felt for the first time completely out of place, but also the weight and hollowness of a country in pain, and our own sterility in being there.

DEATH OF A CURRENCY

Malika came with a cardboard box,
her face pained as though being
forced to eat something unsavoury.
She laid it on our kitchen table
where it rattled with the obstinate
tremors of a fallen regime.

Inside were stacks and rows of
perfectly bundled Soviet rubles,
desperate to escape their obsoletion.

We felt her embarrassment but also her
uncertain fear, and apologetically
exchanged only 50 American dollars'
worth: more than enough to get us to
Tashkent.

One month later they were worthless,
and we had not saved one single soul.

FIVE QUESTIONS REGARDING THE GAP IN THE VEIL

And it was about the sixth hour,
and there was a darkness over the earth
until the ninth hour. And the sun
was darkened, and the veil of the temple
was rent in the midst.
(Luke 23:44,45)

[Eloi Eloi lama sabachthani]

1. Being there in that moment, when
   the earth shook and the rocks split;
   besides an expressway to God,
   what else crept into (out of) that void?

2. Did the abolishment of law create
   more depravity, a [sin] tax haven;
   a morality swear-jar depository for
   the self-righteous and a license to exorcise
   accountability for our black souls?

3. When darkness fell in those hours,
   did all the demons creep up from the abyss,
   stealing past the temple gates to pose as
   philosophers, prophets and priests, setting
   good intentions afire and holding
   the head of peace under an insurmountable
   ocean of blood and water?

4. Did Christ have enough time to do
   what he needed to do while on the other side?

5. If we claim to be righteous,
   who the fuck do we think we are?

PREACHERS SHOULD NOT BE NARCISSISTS

Nor should they harbour eyes of
adultery, setting church walls on fire;
nor take advantage of a man
in his sleep, betraying friendship for lust,
nor conspire to tear families apart,
setting one soul against another in
a subterfuge of self preservation.

These should not read from the Book of
Samuel, lest they be exposed in the sins
of King David: adultery, murder, yet
somehow blessed by God; nor should they
counsel the young that their fleshly desires
are of the earth, that their bodies are
shameful, thereby creating a Frankenstein's
laboratory for warped and twisted futures.

I wonder about Uriah the Hittite: is he
looking down, remembering Bathsheba,
woefully shaking his head?

SACRAMENT

I never understood why we celebrated
the brutal killing of Jesus,
even drawing out the methods and
minute details of his torture like
the worst Brothers Grimm tale ever written;
why not tell the kids instead
about a sparrow that lit upon his shoulder,
reciting soothing poems in his last hour,
or tell of an olive tree that grew
from the tears of Mary Magdalene
huddled at the foot of the cross?
but no, instead we drink blood,
pointing self righteous fingers at
haughty Jews and Romans
at the same time crying out,
thank you, we deserve the punishment!
then declaring on the third day:
see? you can't keep us down,
we are invincible! we are absolved!
singing praises before going home
safely in our cars, driving quickly past
the homeless and the prostitutes
to take off our pious suits and Sunday masks
in time to catch the game,
avoiding our neighbours and our children,
waiting to gorge on sanctified meat.

CHRIST/CHAOS

Whitewashed;
my lines eroded around their moral edges.

[Chaos tumbling following around
every corner, into each hollow]

I took that hard eraser, rubbed myself
down to a

[ecdysis set in motion leaving
never stopping pursuit of righteousness and]

useless
nub,

[little piles of my past to be despised
put your desires in a hole I am a stained creature]

leaving a raw smear of my genesis
still leaking out from under the church door.

[born of sin shed my twisted nature why
I'm just a Frankenstein monster]

Now don't tell me there's no God, sir,
I'm a child of God and He has plans for me;

[I am chaos born of sin
I am]

in fact if Christ was here now, in the flesh,
I think we'd be best friends.

PART 3

THE LOVE POEMS

*(For without love, what are we
but a pile of meat and bones?)*

WHAT LOVE IS

(it's the first time we, as trilobites,
chose to grow eyes and see the world)

(it's when we, before we were birds,
fell out of trees and decided to sprout feathers)

(it's the first time we tasted blood by mistake
and honed our senses for carnivorism)

now, we see in rainbows but demand
to be seen in all the invisible spectrums, too—

we are all coloured in differently,
some with oils, some with encaustic,
some with blackened vine

some keep love enshrined
behind a holy veil; others
fall in love with everyone they meet,

even if just a little.

LOVE IN 31 SYLLABLES

The feel of your breath
in my ear, so tenderly;
'I love you,' you said

Without thinking about it,
I asked which part you loved most

MORE LOVE IN 31 SYLLABLES

'Unfettered,' you said
The sunlight feel of your skin,
each kiss a blossom

Your orchid feet touch my back;
a garden of ecstasy

LOVE IN 17 SYLLABLES

The only sound heard
is a left-handed scribble:
your name on my heart

MORE LOVE IN 17 SYLLABLES

I will take your hand
place on it the long promise
forever to love

AUTUMN MORNING LIGHT

The kitchen window faces west,
painting the red kettle blue.
Unwashed pots and pans gleam softly
of last night's comfort food;
two martini glasses, the ones we rescued
from the antiques market in Ladysmith,
converse at the sink's edge, still ringing
with laughter and certain futures.

Even in the changing light,
this feels like home.

BEING TOGETHER

Our shoes nest as chickens in the front entry closet
Books, once mine and yours, now snuggle on the bookshelves
Me, learning to love old British crime dramas
    and you, watching science fiction films with me (but only the good ones)
Taking turns laying out our nightly supplements
Listening to herons sing pterodactyl lullabies through our bedroom window
Sitting in silence for hours as individuals and then
    being satisfied with the touch of a hand on long walks
Reading to you until you fall asleep

SHE

She borrows fortitude from
her great-grandmother's eye patch,
a rebellion she carries on the inside.

She has survived all the unsurvivable tests,
reassembling herself as a Valkyrie,
not without fear but rife with valour.

She whispers the names of horses,
who in turn still hear and turn their heads
high on the Hat Creek ridge at daybreak.

She has slain the hubris of men
trapped with her inside a boardroom;
logic and reason are her sword and shield.

She finds her peace in the garden,
feeding robins from her own hand
and building houses for bees.

She is the keeper of my heart;
childhood friend, now trusted lover
(my safe place).

SKIN

The skin | to hold a hand, to
we | kiss a cheek, to
live | reach for a friend or
in | hold up the weak;
is not infallible, not | what is touch if not
eternal, not incorruptible, | medicine?
not clean nor pristine; | If not wisdom?
are we not all animals with | If not salvation;
broken down cell walls in | freedom?
radical freefall? | Touch me and feel
Perhaps, however, | my heart beat.
at least somewhat | Touch me and see
inimitable, | that I am real.
at least loveable, | Touch me,
huggable, liveable! | heal me,
For what is skin but | set
an antidote, a | me
power within | free.

VENUS STILLS HER HAND (MENOPAUSE PART 1)

Venus
stills her hand
while young sirens permeate my dreams
I wait for her
as she waits for healing
beautiful in her searching
fierce in her solidarity

LOVING IN ALL THE WAYS

In Greek, there are seven words for love.

A girl once sat me on the edge of a bathtub
and washed my feet, insisting I do nothing in return.

It was the most intimate act of love I have ever received.

Conversely, my greatest act of self love
(decades later) was to utter the words:
'I love you but I can't be with you anymore.'

Is it due to personal loss
that I always cry at the happy things?

Now, after braving volcanoes and glaciers alike,
I understand the apostle Paul when he wrote
that real love transcends feelings or emotion,

but no one ever asks how Jesus really felt when
Mary Magdalene knelt and washed his feet with her hair.

If I could place my hand on his shoulder
perhaps he might tell me of his broken heart,

and I could tell him how lucky I am
to count myself among the mortals,
having the chance to love in all the ways.

THE GRAND CLIMACTERIC (MENOPAUSE PART 2)

men·o·pause
/ˈmenəˌpôz/
(noun: the ceasing of menstruation)

The wisdom written on her face reads like
War and Peace, and she carries maps
in her heart of every nation she's traversed.

Now, the young still shining in her oceanic eyes
begs mercy from a blood moon:
     one more season,
     else be swift.

Her body grows teeth in unexpected places
(she is helpless against its bite)

and I, a spectator in the high seats, also
feel like an exile,
that I can only reflect her brilliance,

offering my hand as we become explorers;
co-cartographers charting
new maps in a foreign place.

PART 4

LAST OF THE MARLBORO MEN

(Once through the Hall of Infinite Doors,
who is worthy to judge; to say
whether or not we've chosen wisely?)

HOW IT MADE ME FEEL THE FIRST TIME I THOUGHT I WAS IN LOVE

like when I, as a teenager
and an expert in the techniques of
Bruce Lee and Jackie Chan,

thought I could punch through
a pane of glass without getting cut

or when, with my best friend's .22,
we shot straight at the hard steel cap
of a tipped oil drum, not for a moment
thinking of the bullet's ricochet

or that time when I as a young boy
had to ask Father to retrieve
my arrow from the pigeon's nest
high in the barn rafters,

and him, seeing I was visibly upset,
reassuring me, saying: *It's ok,*
they shit all over everything anyways.

MEN AND WOMEN

A man is measured by
the size of his penis
or the size of the fish he's holding.
A group of them is called a heroicism;
whatever your problem, they'll fix you.

While the gaggle of girls goes about
stabbing each other in the back,
<give us wine and we'll tell all>
the heroic men sort them out
according to breast size.

(But everyone knows there's nothing
more dangerous than a smart blonde.)

FLOATING, WAITING

floating in space
waiting, in stasis   *[I keep floating off]*

my arm patch of passion
(*once brilliant*)
now faded; now jaded   *[... visor is completely fogged,*
nearly frozen to me]

I think I'll die soon
suspended in this vacuum   *[I can't get over there]*
me and Major Tom

(Somebody get me   *[I can't get to where I want]*
Chris Hadfield on Zoom)

[you'll have to leave me out here]

ALGORITHM

sort/shuffle
filter visual input for
short code: see
not the whole face
but scan relative data points;
<blonde, caucasian, tall>
wait for the turn of the head,
sift through lightning bolts for
relevant comparisons:
pain points [safe memory]
    will this person
harm me/affect me/make me
love myself/make me
feel threatened/hold any
promise of connection/
    wait, did I hear what they just said?

ALGORITHM 2 (SIGNAL TO NOISE)

divided
binary switch flipped
my coded thumb on autoslip
yes I heard you
[goddamn that Joe D is lit]
I don't know/what did you want/
I'm listening! (look up quick)
[whoa scroll past that
before I get nicked]
ok sounds good/next week/got it
[hang on, new follower!]
that's tomorrow?/
I'll put it in my calendar/
[replying: heart heart flower]
can we talk about it later?/
or best yet/just text it

THE MALE GAZE

I forgot to warn my sons about their eyes.

When I look at Yuko Shimizu's painting
Dusting Off the Male Gaze
I can't help but feel guilt.

Paper cutouts of my careless glances
litter cafés and sidewalks;
latent evidence of my man crimes
left in blatant black and red outlines,

and even though I see Free Love
beginning a new renaissance, sprouting up
through these Gen-X ashes,
I still feel the urge to apologize.

MY WARP & MY WEFT

My right hand swells with abuse;
a bludgeon for my own fabric making.
If I think of this, my distorted lines
seem less painful.

> *Like the tall grass at a high school party*
> *where a drunken friend asked me to take*
> *her virginity, my weave frays at the edges.*
> *I said no, and live with the unknown.*

Now, my wefts, as the lines around my eyes,
have become loose, drooping with time.
If I focus on this I may not notice
the memories that occasionally show through.

> *Like the skirt another coached me to pull up*
> *because it was too tight to pull down, my warp*
> *still yanks on the corners of my mouth.*
> *I did not say no, and live with regret.*

Are the rooms behind me full, or
do I empty them out as I make each new
garment, pulling my regrets along in
a charivari of trailing wedding cans?

> *My childhood blanket is long worn through,*
> *yet it still shouts out lies of innocence;*
> *I know this to be true because I still*
> *feel embarrassed every time I touch myself.*

THE SENSITIVE MALE

As a male writer I must be cautious, for
in exploring the labyrinth of consciousness
I might be tempted to reveal
secreted aspects of my flawed masculinity,
or raw personal histories of my gender,

> *[my first wet dream involved a geisha,*
> *I remember it vividly;*
> *it was my only untainted sexual experience]*

or weaknesses meant to be covered over
by small man excuses and smaller man lies.

> *[I asked mother about it and she covered*
> *my mouth; that is when I knew shame]*

Like posies, I carry a pocket full of confidence.
However as a man I must hide my alter-ego,
the half-constructed superego, the guilt
that I wear as a bloody sheep-skinned cloak.

> *[I overheard a man say that looking at*
> *a pretty girl is like looking at the sun:*
> *look too long and it may burn your eyes]*

Along with the fires of lust I must brandish
an extinguisher with which to put them out
lest I be censored, excommunicated, pitied;
judged as just another pig.

> *[Tonight I will sleep in the forest. There,*
> *I can be safe from myself]*

A friend once called me a S.N.A.G. and
I asked her what it meant. 'It's from the sixties,'
she said; 'Sensitive New Age Guy.'
But I would never pin it on my chest as my pronoun.

LAST OF THE MARLBORO MEN

I was not a man in the seventies
back when being a man was easy.

The eighties brought confusion, with
Mick Dundee sorting genders by hand
on the big screen while we laughed,

and all the kids in gym class forming
a predatory circle around Paul Mitchell when
he got a boner in the boy's change room.

(My father's sex advice was always framed
in jokes and metaphors; he thought he was
doing a good job, but it made me sad for him.)

No, I learned about manhood when
I became married in '91: it was the year the first
of the Marlboro Men died of lung cancer.

Now my children teach me about gender
equality and the proper use of pronouns.

In a quagmire of embarrassments,
I can guarantee my father never heard
the word *cisgender* and I, no Marlboro Man
in me, am still learning what it means.

TUTORIAL FOR AGING

Put your passions in a trunk; some things
are better left for reminiscing.
Be more opinionated.
Paint your walls grey instead of
going outside in the rain.
Never ask for help, better to face it alone.
Look, but don't touch.
Relegate that new spot on your
left temple to a sinister badge of tenure.
Give up grooming incrementally
because no one notices anyways.
Understand that your body is a time bomb,
and forget the rush of dancing in a club;
these things must only be done in private.
(Do not believe the propaganda songs
that would paint you as a god.)
Don't try too hard for anything, lest
it be perceived as sad.

FEAR OF AGING BADLY

heed the season:
faint pithy flesh and compost—

(I miss your whimpers,
your trembling limbs like aspens,
but we are dry leaves in
the long autumn)

how unfair the poisoned root
scorched and unwound early
no blossoms in spring
no low-hanging promise of fruit

so we lie
still, among ourselves
pass days feigning love
as *National Geographic*,

binge watching till the end
(only) waiting for tender shoots
to grow back and
fill our nostrils

AS THE TRILLIUM

I see the young faces and
recognize myself in them,
the white petals of newness
planting prepared fields
    for future.

I feel the boy inside pushing
at the edges, calling out:
the time is ripe/seize the day!
Happiness swells at the sight
    of promise.

But am I being foolish to
risk a smile, knowing
my whitening beard betrays me,
as one who passes on fields of
    stalks and dust?

Like the trillium
at the end of its years, is my
face darkening at pace with
the poisoned earth, turning
    purple with fatigue?

in the right light
I'm a magnificent orchid;
not magnificent like one of
Mapplethorpe's orchids—
nothing to proudly display
on a gallery wall or
family calendar or
even an IG selfie
(they look like they feel passion,
those flowers, like
I used to feel passion)
my leaves may be
a bit leathery and spotted,
my roots a tad dehydrated,
and I may be dropping
a few petals but damn;
    [in a distorted]
    [quarter-second]
    [parking lot]
    [rear-view mirror snapshot]
I'm still a magnificent orchid

MAPPLETHORPE ORCHID

PART 5

REQUIEM

*(It is a good thing
to weigh one's own history carefully,
sorting truth from fiction
and wheat from chaff.)*

PORCINE MAN

In 1978 my dad killed a pig with a sledgehammer.

I was nine then; it was the first time
I felt the sideways tilting of the earth.
I thought if I ran fast enough
I could reverse time, or maybe at least
shed my poisoned skin to purge
the red devil that he birthed that day.
Lost were pinwheels or model robots;
the monster under my bed became real,
singing his slow hollow sounds of death.
Whenever I looked at my dad after that,
his face seemed rounder, his nose
a bit longer, more porcine.
Respect shifted into a hidden room
and never returned; a role model lost
together with my naive childhood faith
that we could all be good,
that we could all be kind.

THE ART OF BOX MAKING

They say that life is preserved in the grain of wood;
that each piece carries the history of the earth within,
connected somehow to the very first seeds of creation.

To bring out that grain for human contemplation via
hand plane and scraper, or fine sanding
followed by a penetrating oil then wax

is a religious act; incorporating keyed mitres,
finger joints, or three or four-way grain matching
brings one to the level of re-creator,

an engaged partner in the story of life itself.
But what you will not learn at the School of Woodworking
is how much spirit to put into your father's urn

nor how much to hold back,
knowing that when you place his ashes inside, he too
will become part of the history of the earth,

taking a part of you with him.

NIGHT SWEATS

ten
cruel, cold
curled fingers of sleep
tattoo bruises on my psyche
laughing as death unfurls, casting
me off the roof in comedic zoetrope loops
like charlie chaplin endlessly chasing his bowler
even my dog falls and I trip trying to save her
I search so frantically for an escape that
my dead father rises from his ragged
compost heap to hold up his
massive hand and say,
stop all of your
failing,
boy

TWO-HEADED REFLECTION OF MYSELF

if you were
still here, would we
sit and chat over coffee,
comparing illnesses and in-
juries and offering up insights
to the work at hand? would you
tell me of mistakes you've made,
boast of feats of great strength,
or speak softly about your short
comings as a father? I wonder if,
now that I've surpassed your age,
we would be friends on an equal basis,
although I feel so much younger than
you yet so much older at the same time.
would I see myself in you, or you
in me, keeping the best parts of
us both, or would it simply be a
misshapen two-headed reflection? if you were still here
would I take the time to visit
you or would I
make excuses
and avoid you
because I don't
really want to know?

THIS IS NOT YOUR[MY] LIFE

My father's hands
hang, reanimated,
at the ends of my arms.
Massive, calloused, stained
with transgression,
identical twins to the leather gauntlets
left frozen in the shape of generations,
now facing me[us] on his[my] workbench.
I[we] sit there, conjuring wagers,
flexing alien fingers to reveal
a jack of spades, curled and sweaty;
a bid to put the family zeitgeist to bed.
I[we] hear his[my] hoarse voice gurgle up
from the grave of [his]my throat:

<<CALL>>

and I[we] know I[we] should've gone all in but
lack the courage for consequence.
I[we] know that this is not his[my] beautiful house
this is not his[my] tranquil life, yet
somehow the high card never falls to me[us].
His[my] phantom eye drips contempt on the table
as I[we] make my[our] final play:

<Thanks for all the life lessons, Dad, but
when I[we] become old, I[we]
will be referred to as *gentleman*.>

FAMILY SPIRIT

I had only heard about my
uncle's black foot, which is
probably worse than if I'd
actually seen it;
the monster I imagined
eating at his limbs
still lives in my head.
(All of my uncles are dead now,
and I wait to see
which of their monsters
will come for me.)
Will my fate be more severe
because I didn't attend
any of their funerals, or
is the seal of my curse simply that,
like magnets, our family spirit
attracts destruction?

REQUIEM

                              a cello
              exhales a requiem in E minor,
          low and melancholy; calling out
                  to all the forgotten spirits;
          I know it must be meant for me
                  by the bitter taste of
              iron filings on my tongue
      and how my body pulls to the earth
                      when I hear it.
                today, it sings softly
      but the melody grows louder in this
                      hidden garden
with every inescapable passing hour,
              the vibrato announcing:
              [you, too, will end]

DREAMING OF GETTING DRUNK WITH MY DAD AT A WEDDING

Maybe, as a last-ditch bridge,
Dad and I could have gotten drunk together
at least once, at a wedding maybe,
or at a karaoke bar singing
all the gospel songs we used to sing
as a family group at church when I was little.
    (Daddy sang bass, Momma sang tenor,
    me 'n little brother would join right in there
    in the sky, Lord, in the sky...)
I can still do harmony but I think maybe
I'm too old for the tambourine now;
in fact perhaps we could form a
barbershop quartet with all the uncles,
getting drunk together and discussing
family matters like *why no one told me how to be a man*
and I could tell them sorry for avoiding you
but I had nothing to say; maybe I still don't but
at least we can get drunk together and sing,
maybe, and I can play tambourine to keep time
and harmonize, to try to hold it all together,
and maybe between them all, they can help me out
with how I'm supposed to act around the people
I love, like maybe somehow it was supposed to be easy;
something like, *be good*, or *be kind to one another*,
but at the very least maybe we could just get drunk and sing.

HOMESTEAD

I wonder if I went back
to the old homestead, the mill now gone
and the Great Garden beside the curving
two-track lane reverted back to bramble,
would there be anything left to feel;
a grasping of straws for a settling of accounts?
I wonder if the back fields, two liver-shaped
parcels framed in wilderness, would still be visible
from the upstairs window, or if it would
all now be mowed down into
one sterile clearing devoid of resident
porcupines or deer or curious bears.
I wonder if I'd still be able to recognize
my father's fingerprints in the sworls
of the now-weathered spruce siding that we'd
harvested from the property with horses
and cut on the mill that he made with his own hands,
or if his scent might still linger in the air there.
I wonder if I would recognize myself in hindsight
and reach out to explain the things
that I did not understand then.

REMEMBERING HIS FACE

one snowflake, a single
lemon drop on the tip of
the outstretched tongue,
a childhood door pried open, beckoning
warmly that place in a cold country,
one piece of flying ash, glowing
ember to illuminate
one word, one thought, one
memory a single layer deep,
one passing notion or
momentary flash of his face
that can't be isolated,
a billion snowflakes swirling
among the ashes
in a cold northern wind.

ROOTS

I tried searching on Google Earth
for the farm I grew up on in Ontario
for a quick look back at my roots,

(I couldn't find it)

and I can't say that nothing stays the same when
there is no evidence of history;
I didn't know my grandmothers either,

which is a consequence of living in a large country,
like our old farmhouse in Ontario
was a large country, and I realised too late

after my own home became
a foreign country laced with landmines,
that roots are as fleeting as the ground beneath us;

always changing, sometimes tilting or
suddenly opening up to swallow us,
that *roots* is merely a metaphor for *belonging.*

Thank you

To my amazing partner Carmen for her undying encouragement and patience with me as I continue to pursue creative projects.

To Jan Miklaszewicz for his keen editor's eye, keeping me from going too 'cowboy' with my punctuation...

To the many poets and artists whom I've befriended both locally and online.

Acknowledgements

"Tijuana" previously published in *Anthology II*, (2021) by Poets Against Poverty

"The Art of Box Making", previously published in the anthology *No Man's Land*, (2022) curated and edited by Jan Miklaszewicz

Scott Hamilton spent his early formative years on a farm in southern Ontario. When he was eleven years old his family moved to an undeveloped plot of land in northern British Columbia with the intent of homesteading. He attended Emily Carr College of Art and Design in Vancouver before becoming a carpenter and cabinet maker. Scott now resides on Vancouver Island, BC. His work has appeared in several anthologies; *Last of the Marlboro Men* is his first book.

To learn more visit: www.scottahamilton.com

CPSIA information can be obtained
at www.ICGtesting.com
Printed in the USA
LVHW110435121022
730468LV00005B/251

9 781778 281006